INVENTIONS

KFK KINGFISHER KNOWLEDGE

INVENTIONS

James Robinson

Foreword by
James Dyson

KINGFISHER

Senior editors: Simon Holland, Hannah Wilson
Senior designer: Peter Clayman
Picture research manager: Cee Weston-Baker
Picture researcher: Rachael Swann
Senior production controller: Lindsey Scott
DTP manager: Nicky Studdart
Indexer and proof-reader: Carron Brown

GO FURTHER...
INFORMATION PANEL KEY:

websites and further reading

career paths

places to visit

KINGFISHER

Kingfisher Publications Plc, New Penderel House,
283–288 High Holborn, London WC1V 7HZ
www.kingfisherpub.com

First published by Kingfisher Publications Plc 2006
10 9 8 7 6 5 4 3 2 1

1TR/0606/TWP/MA(MA)/130ENSOMA/F

ISBN-13: 978 0 7534 1322 7
ISBN-10: 0 7534 1322 1

Copyright © Kingfisher Publications Plc 2006

Printed in Singapore

NOTE TO READERS
The website addresses listed in this book are correct at the time of going to print.
However, due to the ever-changing nature of the internet, website addresses and
content can change. Websites can contain links that are unsuitable for children.
The publisher cannot be held responsible for changes in website addresses or
content, or for information obtained through third-party websites. We strongly
advise that internet searches should be supervised by an adult.

Contents

A collection of turbines harnessing
energy from the wind near to
Palm Springs, California, USA

Foreword

At school you are taught English, maths and science, but I imagine few of you have had the good fortune to attend a lesson in invention. If invention classes were taught in school, they would, I think, be very popular. Just imagine... 'In today's lesson we are going to learn how to invent the robot that will do all your homework. Next week we will be creating the contraption that will transport you from your home to school with a snap of a finger.' It's the stuff of science fiction!

As it stands, invention is shrouded in mystery. Perhaps you've heard the story of Archimedes, the ancient Greek mathematician, who had a flash of inspiration and solved a long-pondered problem while taking a bath. Famously he cried 'Eureka!' (which means 'I have found it') and ran, stark-naked, through the streets. As a child I was told this legendary tale of scientific discovery – and a magical story it is, too! The problem, though, is it makes invention seem just like... magic. And unless you're Harry Potter, magic is not something that you can easily learn at school. Fortunately, however, for most engineers and scientists invention is much more a case of experimentation, of trial and error. Sure, there are occasional sparks of genius, but mostly a new invention comes down to a curious mind, determination and creativity – something that you all have.

Whether you are interested in the invention of aeroplanes, robots, nanotechnology or even vacuum cleaners, the starting point is always frustrations and problems. In the case of aeroplanes, for example, why are we earth-bound in our transportation? Why can't we copy the elegance, speed and freedom of, say, birds? Why can't we fly? In my case, I started by asking questions such as, 'why do vacuum cleaners fail to do the job for which they were designed?' 'Why do they lose suction?'

From frustration, the next step is working out the cause of the problem. Here, I recommend a hands-on approach – take things apart! When I was faced with the problem of the offending hoover, I decided to cut it open and find out exactly what was causing the problem. So, where next? Well, it's at this point that a so-called 'Eureka' moment can come in useful. You need an idea. My idea was to do away with the vacuum cleaner bag and replace it with a cyclone, which proved to be a much better way of sucking up dust.

But an inkling of an idea is just the starting point. Trial and error is the key to transforming the spark into a reality. My first, very crude, prototype was simply made from cardboard and gaffer tape attached to the body of my old vacuum cleaner. This was the first step in a long process of developing my invention. There were 5,126 more prototypes before my invention was complete. So think about this the next time you phone a friend on a mobile phone, listen to music on your shiny new MP3 player or ride in a car. While these inventions do amazing things with apparent ease, behind each one there are people like me, taking things apart, testing things out, trying something new, having fun. Why don't you try it, too?

James Dyson

James Dyson, design-engineer and inventor of the cyclone vacuum cleaner, the Sea Truck Boat and the Evolutionary Ballbarrow

Coloured X-ray of
a computer monitor

CHAPTER 1

Communications

We live in a chatty, noisy world of communications. We cannot do anything without exchanging words, radio signals or data. Our homes and offices are filled with telephones, fax machines and computers with email. And our pockets jangle with mobile phones and keys that send out tiny radio messages to open car doors. Yet a century ago, communications meant the tapping of Morse code, the smudgy ink of newspapers or the scratch of a pen.

A torrent of clever inventions changed all that. Communications became popular and then essential to our lives. Today, we keep information moving on a global web of wires and waves. Communications satellites soar above us and, beneath our feet, optical fibres glow with data, carrying information faster than a blink of an eye. Even when we tire of talking, texting and emailing, it is the communications industry that entertains us, as we tune in to movies, television and radio channels.

The telephone

A musical ring from your pocket. Maybe it is that call you have been waiting for? You hit the talk button: 'Hi!' Making calls on the move or sending a text – even to another country – is so easy we take it for granted. It is no longer unusual to watch a movie on a phone or to pick up email from one. Until 1978, however, technology was not advanced enough even to make a mobile call around the corner – let alone around the world. Earlier phones all trailed a cable linking them to the tangle of wires that connected calls.

▲ Early telephones, like this 'candlestick' model from 1913, had a separate mouthpiece and earpiece, and no dial. Callers spoke into the microphone on top of the stick, and listened through the earpiece. Dialling numbers was impossible – instead people spoke to an operator, who connected calls by pushing plugs into the correct sockets at the telephone exchange.

Telegraphy

Amazingly, this network of wires came before telephones themselves. The wires buzzed not with voices, but with 'Morse code' – an alphabet of short and long electric pulses. This method of sending messages was called telegraphy. The first person to send a voice down a telegraph wire was Italian-American Antonio Meucci (1808–96). His lack of English and his poverty prevented him from developing his invention. Scottish-American teacher Alexander Graham Bell (1847–1922) created the first practical telephone system in 1876.

The first mobile phones

By the 1950s, undersea cables linked telephones around the world, but in other ways phones hardly changed until the invention of mobiles some 30 years ago. The first handsets were the size of bricks. They beamed calls to antennae on nearby phone masts, which were linked to regular telephone lines. Each antenna provided calls to one 'cell' (a small area of good reception), so the new phones were called cell-phones. By 1991, cheaper, tinier computer chips made possible the digital mobiles we use today.

▼ Today's mobile phones are small and compact with built-in aerials. Many of them double up as cameras and allow us to send photographs across the air waves.

▲ A mobile phone can be a useful piece of safety equipment because if you are lost or injured, you can call for help. But remember — often there is no reception in remote regions. Many people live in areas so remote that telephone wires have never reached them. Mobile phones may at last take calls to these distant corners of the world, because building just one tall antenna to serve a whole village is cheaper than running telephone wires to every single house.

The future of phones

In wealthier, well-connected nations, phones keep getting cheaper, smaller and smarter. Picture and movie calls are already common, and tomorrow's phones will perform the same functions as small computers. Linked to the internet, they will let you control your home from afar. You will be able to program the TV, turn on the heating, and let the cat out — all from your handset. Perhaps you will even use it to make calls, too!

Fibre optics

Inside a glowing glass thread, 10,000 telephone conversations buzz. These threads of glass, each the thickness of a human hair, are called optical fibres. Lying on the seabed, they relay phone calls and data between continents. In the city streets, they bring a hundred TV channels into homes. Fibre optics, which is the transmission of information through optical fibres, works by guiding beams of light. Smart electronics crams data into each glowing beam. Reflected from the fibre's shiny walls, the beam travels many kilometres without losing strength.

▲ Inside a fibre-optic communications cable there is a bundle of optical fibres. In this picture, which is six times larger than actual size, the dark circles are fibres that are out of use and carrying no data.

Bouncing light

Compared to the copper wires they replace, fibre optics are cheaper, more reliable, and carry more information faster. Fibre optics have these remarkable qualities because each has a perfectly clear core. A very shiny cladding (wrapping) gives the fibre a mirror-like coating. Light shining in at one end bounces endlessly along, no matter how the fibre is bent or twisted. To send information down a fibre, computers first turn it into digital form – a string of on-off signals. These power a laser at the end of the fibre, flashing the beam quickly on and off. Circuits at the other end change the pulsing light back into an electric current.

protective jacket

strength layer

cladding

optical fibre

▲ A fibre-optic communications cable contains optical fibres wrapped in several protective layers. The cladding around each fibre creates the mirror-like surface to keep light from spilling out. A strength layer wraps up all the fibres, ensuring that they do not snap during installation. Finally, an outer plastic jacket protects the cable and keeps water out.

Illuminating water

Fibre optics did not start as a way of sending messages, and the first experiments used water, not glass threads. In 1870, British physicist John Tyndall (1820–93) showed that by lighting up a jar of water, he could make the light run along a curving jet flowing from a hole in the jar. In other words, he discovered that the outside of the jet of water acted as a mirror, reflecting light within the flowing stream. Fibre optics lit up aircraft cockpit dials from the 1920s, but the first fibre-optic communications cable was not laid until 1977.

The many uses of fibre optics

Today, most fibre optics are used in communications, but they do many other jobs, too. In hospitals, a bundle of fibres with a lens at each end is called an endoscope. It allows surgeons to peer inside a patient's body. Extra fibres carry a light beam to brighten the darkness inside the lungs or guts. The fibres' bendiness lets them turn the tightest of the body's corners. Engineers use similar devices to look inside sewer pipes or parts of aircraft that are normally hidden from view.

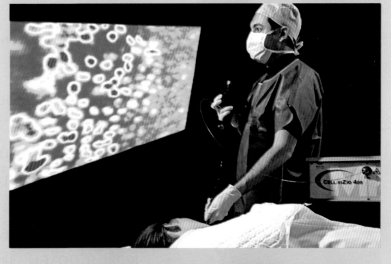

▲ Using optical fibres, doctors can put a microscope right inside the human body. They guide a probe, just one-third of the size of a human hair, towards diseased tissues. Then the 'Cell-viZio device' displays greatly magnified images from the probe on a computer screen.

Communications satellites

Next time you are outside just after dusk or before dawn on a clear, dark night, look upwards. You may see a tiny pinprick of light moving quickly across the sky. It is not a star. It is not an aircraft. It is a satellite, circling Earth thousands of kilometres above your head. Satellites play a major part in communications. They provide us with television channels, phone calls and internet connections. Satellites do other jobs, too. Some watch the weather or the stars, guide travellers or act as 'spies in the skies'.

◄ This weather satellite is observing a hurricane on Earth. Like most communications satellites today, it is 'geostationary' because it appears to hover motionlessly above Earth. The satellites that you see moving across the night sky circle Earth much more quickly and are in lower orbits.

▲ This photograph, taken in 1962, shows technicians in New York testing the *Telstar* satellite a few days before it was launched into space. *Telstar* was the first communications satellite and it carried TV pictures and phone calls across the Atlantic Ocean between the USA and Europe.

Geostationary satellites

These satellites were the idea of English science-fiction writer Arthur C Clarke (born 1917). Geostationary satellites would appear to be stationary (not moving) because they would orbit (travel around) Earth at the same speed as it rotates. The rotation of Earth takes exactly one day and the satellites would also take 24 hours to complete their orbit. In 1945, when space exploration was impossible, Clarke suggested that such satellites might provide a cheap, worldwide TV system. Clarke's dream came true less than 20 years later. The first geostationary satellite, *Syncom 2*, was launched in 1963. It broadcast TV to half the world.

▼ The very first communications satellites used radio telescopes like this one in Hawaii, USA, as receiving dishes. Today, many dishes are less than one metre wide.

The ups and downs of satellite signals

Communications satellites work like a 'Chinese whispers' game. They receive microwave signals broadcast from an uplink station on one side of Earth. Then they 'pass it on' to a downlink station on the other side. Uplink and downlink stations are not always far apart. Satellite TV is often broadcast from an uplink station (usually a big satellite dish) in the same country as the people watching. The downlink stations are the small dishes on their houses.

Satellite navigation

Today, we rely on satellites for many things besides TV. The global positioning system (GPS) uses 24 low-orbit satellites to broadcast navigation signals. Sailors, pilots, drivers and hikers use the signals to find out where they are. 'Looking satellites' have discovered new galaxies and they have helped to prove beyond doubt that Earth's climate is warming. Earth observation satellites can be 'spy in the sky' satellites, spotting hidden weapons of war or detecting cheating farmers who cut down protected forests.

▼ This photographer, working in the foothills of Mount Everest, is using a portable satellite receiver dish to exchange conversations and pictures with his colleagues in London, UK. For conversations only, satellite phones not much bigger than normal mobiles can be used.

Computers

How many computers do you use each day? If you think it is just one or two, think again. It is more likely to be at least a dozen. The PC you use to do your homework, send email or surf the web is just the start. Smart, fast computers run your mobile phone and if you draw money from a cash machine, you are using a whole network of connected computers. Even your toaster or washing machine probably has a computer chip inside. Without computers, our familiar, comfortable world would grind to a halt.

Mechanical computers

The first computers whirred and clunked with brass gear wheels. They were the invention of English maths genius Charles Babbage (1792–1871). Babbage's machines were tricky to build, however, and computers did not succeed until electronic parts replaced moving parts. The first device that you might recognize as a computer was built in about 1940 by Bulgarian-American scientist John Atanasoff (1903–95). Like today's machines, it worked digitally, using a 'binary' system that stored and added numbers as a series of on/off (one/zero) electric pulses.

▲ To create the microprocessors that power modern computers, engineers etch a pattern of tiny components on a chip of silicon using a photographic process. This microprocessor is small enough to fit on an adult's thumbnail, yet it contains 1,350,000 transistors. It is 1,000 times more powerful than the room-sized *Colossus* computer (right), which was built 50 years earlier.

▲ This is *Colossus*, the first electronic digital computer. It was developed by the British in 1943, during World War II, to try to translate coded messages by the Germans. Like all early computers, *Colossus* was huge and heavy and, according to the magazine *Popular Mechanics*, this was not going to change: in 1949, the magazine reported that 'Computers in the future may weigh no more than 1.5 tons'.

▲ Cheap and tiny, computer chips can now even control and guide toys. These Aquaroid swimming robots, launched in Japan in 2000, use computer guidance to mimic the behaviour of real aquarium fish.

Size matters

In the late 1950s, computers began to get smaller when hot glass valves were replaced by transistors – devices that increase or switch an electrical current. The integrated circuit, invented in about 1960, squeezed hundreds (later millions) of transistors onto a single tiny chip. This helped computers to shrink to the size of a refrigerator by the mid 1960s. The first home computers, which appeared about ten years later, were about the same size as modern home or office computers. Today, we are obsessed with size and portability – laptops are not much bigger than a sheet of A4 paper and your mobile phone is a sophisticated computer that can fit in the palm of your hand.

Quantum computers

Although today's computers still perform calculations with the binary system, this could soon change. Quantum computers use the properties of the tiniest particles to add, subtract and store numbers. Defying common sense, these small particles can be in several places at once, so each one can store many numbers. Quantum computers are fiendishly hard to build, but they will be faster and more powerful than any machine we use today.

▼ An architect uses CAD (computer-aided design) software to plan the construction of an oil refinery.

The internet

It spans every country in the world; 500 million people use it each week; it doubles in size every year. The internet is vast, valuable and spreading, but what exactly is it? It's a way of connecting computers, and a set of rules to control how they talk to each other. Devised in the USA in the 1950s as a way to launch nuclear weapons, the internet long ago left behind its warlike past. Today, we use it to download music, sell things and keep in touch with friends.

▲ Programmer and computer scientist Tim Berners-Lee dreamt of an easy-to-use program that would let him find and read many different kinds of data, no matter where and how it was stored on the internet. Berners-Lee's first words-only web browser achieved this, but the web got really popular only when later browsers, such as *Mosaic*, made it possible to add pictures.

The birth of the World Wide Web

In 1989, English computer programmer Tim Berners-Lee (born 1955) was working on an international science project in France and Switzerland. He figured out a simple but clever way to link information. Inside pages of text on a computer screen, he hid special codes. The codes highlighted words, showing they were linked to other pages. Clicking on the words changed the page to display the new, linked text. Berners-Lee called his code Hypertext Markup Language (HTML) and the pages that used it the World Wide Web.

◀ Today, people all over the world use the internet without ever really thinking about what it is, or where it is. The web makes this possible, linking together billions of pages of information on millions of computers. The internet existed as a network of connected computers in the 1980s but, until the invention of the web, only scientists and computer experts could use it.

The arrival of email

The web made the internet simple to use, and as more and more people got connected, they discovered another brilliant idea – email. Computer-expert Ray Tomlinson (born 1941) thought up email in 1971. He chose the '@' (at) symbol to separate a computer user's own name from the name of the network that connected him or her to the internet. Together, email and the web made the internet an extraordinary success. By 1993, internet use was doubling roughly each month.

▼ The Google search engine began as a research project at America's Stanford University in 1996 by inventors Sergey Brin (born 1973) and Larry Page (born 1973). It is named after a 'googol' – the number ten multiplied by itself 100 times.

Googling

As the web grew bigger, finding information became harder. Search engines attempted to solve this problem. These software robots follow links between pages, and make a searchable index from the words on each page. The most successful of all search engines, Google, does much more than this. It judges the importance of each page it finds by counting the pages that link to it. Today, Google is so popular that it has become a verb: 'don't give me the web address – I'll just Google it'.

Radio

Turn on a DAB (digital) radio, and you will hear stereo sound without the hiss and crackle that can spoil traditional radio reception. DAB is short for digital audio broadcasting, the technology that makes this possible. DAB uses computer processing to turn sound into a stream of zeroes and ones that arrive at your radio exactly as they were broadcast. A computer inside a DAB radio set turns the digital signal back into music or speech – and can even show song titles, sports scores or station information on a display screen.

▲ Introduced in 1954, transistor radios were small and light enough to carry around, for go-anywhere music. They are still just as popular

Radio stations

Radio as we now know it began on Christmas Eve 1906, when Canadian inventor Reginald Fessenden (1866–1932) broadcast speech and music for the first time. Hardly anyone heard it because radio receivers were still rare and expensive. Popular broadcasts did not begin until 1920, when the radio station KDKA went on the air in the city of Pittsburgh, USA. Just two years later, there were 600 American radio stations. More than one million people tuned in to their broadcasts.

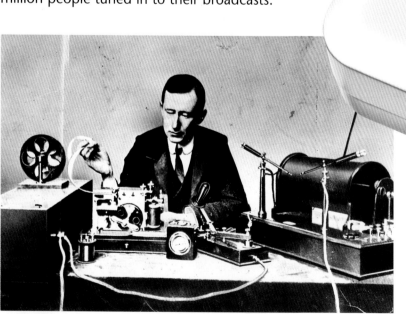

▲ The first radio signals were broadcast in 1894 by Italian student Guglielmo Marconi (1874–1937). His crude transmitter could broadcast only a Morse-code alphabet of short and long crackles. At the time, messages in Morse code were sent along telegraph wires (see page 8) and so Marconi called his invention 'wireless telegraphy'.

▲ Pocket-sized, and no bigger than a pack of playing cards, this DAB radio has a built-in MP3 player and recorder (see page 35). There are buttons to record live radio programmes, and to pause them. A standard-sized cable plugs into the socket on the side for downloading music from a computer.

Entertainment

We are still tuning in. Despite competition from TV, CDs and other kinds of entertainment, radio is very popular. Why? Because countless radio stations provide us with a huge variety of free programmes. And because radio sets work almost anywhere. Some are small enough to fit behind our ears – others you can wind up, for music without batteries.

▶ A wind-up radio is powered by a handle that, when turned, coils up a spring. As the spring slowly unwinds, the radio plays. Solar panels often provide back-up power.

solar panels

crank handle

▲ Trevor Bayliss (born 1937) invented the wind-up radio in 1993. He had watched a TV programme about Africa. Radios were often the only means of communication there, but many people did not have access to electricity or could not afford batteries to power them.

A powerful means of communication

Since its earliest days, radio has been used to hold one-to-one conversations across the world or just around the corner. Taxi drivers and police forces use radio communication because it allows a constant and direct link between two stations – and once the hardware (equipment) has been bought, radio use is free. Today, low-power transmitters and computers make radio even more useful than ever. Radio waves connect computers to printers, scan the barcodes on your shopping, open doors, and make life easier in a million other ways.

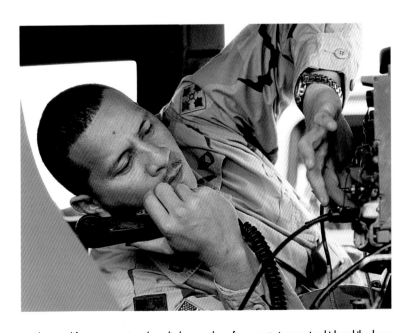

▲ The armed forces communicate by radio because they often operate in areas in which mobile-phone antennae or telephone lines do not exist or have been destroyed. Military radio sets include powerful software that translates conversations into code, preventing information getting into the wrong hands.

Television

Not long ago, watching TV meant wiggling an aerial on top of the set and choosing from only three or four channels. Today, most of us enjoy flicker-free pictures and stereo sound, and may be able to choose from hundreds of channels beamed to us from a satellite. Tomorrow's TVs promise better pictures, and even more choice – once they are wired to the internet, we will be able to throw away the TV guide, and watch what we like, when we like.

▲ In 1926, inventor John Logie Baird showed that TV was possible. TV broadcasts began soon after, but only 30 or so people watched them – on home-made sets. The pictures were blurred, flickering and silent. When regular TV broadcasts began, Baird's spinning-disc system was forgotten.

▼ The first TV shows were broadcast live, just like stage plays. In the USA, shows often featured the sponsor's name or product. As the giant tube suggests, toothpaste paid for this 1951 quiz show 'Strike it Rich'.

The arrival of the television
Scotsman John Logie Baird (1888–1946) was the first to make a working television, though his spinning-disc system gave small, crude pictures. An electronic system invented quite separately in the USA by Philo Farnsworth (1906–71) and Vladimir Zworkin (1889–1982) led to the TV sets we use today. Early pictures were in black-and-white; colour TV broadcasts did not begin until the 1950s.

▲ Look closely at a TV screen – you will see that it is made from thousands of tiny, coloured dots.

Live studio audiences
All early TV was 'live' – viewers watched programmes at the same time as they were happening in the studio. It was not possible to record TV programmes until 1953. The first video recorders were vast machines that used a kilometre of tape for every 100 seconds of programme. Video cassette recorders (VCRs) appeared in the 1970s, and today's digital versatile discs (DVDs) began to replace them 20 years later.

Channel hopping

Television is a big part of our lives: most of us watch it for four hours a day – more time than we spend reading, playing sports or meeting friends, all put together. Fortunately, TV is getting better. Digital broadcasting already squeezes many more TV programmes into the limited number of channels available. New TV sets are all digital, too: they include smart computers that put super-sharp, wide-format images up on their flat screens.

▲ Cable and satellite television stations broadcast hundreds of channels. Advertising pays for many of them; viewers pay to receive many more. Some of the channels appeal to special groups of people, such as anglers or fans of just one football club. These special-interest channels can thrive because new technology has dramatically cut the cost of running a TV channel.

▼ Future TV screens may be flexible, wafer thin, cheap – and printed using ink-jets. Light-emitting polymers (plastics) glow when electricity passes through them. Printed in a grid pattern they can display moving TV pictures.

Going digital

The switch to digital TV also improves the way you control your TV – it will become much easier to choose programmes, watch sports from different angles, buy stuff or vote in on-screen competitions. And because digital TV channels are just computer data, TV stations will deliver over the internet. Very soon, downloads could replace your local video rental store: you will be able to watch almost every movie you have ever heard of – but you will have to pay for them.

Film and cinema

On the movie screen, heroes turn into hideous monsters, astronauts fight wars in space, and dinosaurs come to life to chase terrified scientists. Cinema's special effects look so real it is hard to believe computers created them. Computers can turn a few extras into a vast army, and change a city studio into an Arctic ice-flow or tropical jungle. But film-making was not quite so easy before the arrival of computer animation.

▲ Optical toys, such as this zoetrope from 1834, showed moving pictures before the invention of cinema or even photography. Small drawings, each slightly different, were placed around the inside of a metal drum. Spinning the drum and looking through slits in the side, the viewer saw the pictures one after the other. Each blurred into the next, so that they seemed to move.

Early cinema

In the earliest films, the novelty of a picture moving on a screen was itself so astonishing that special effects were hardly necessary. The first film, shown in 1894 by English inventor William Dickson (1860–1935) and his American employer Thomas Edison (1847–1931) simply featured a barber's shop and a blacksmith, among other subjects. The audience paid 5 cents each to watch the 20-second-long films in a 'kinetoscope', which is a kind of peepshow.

▼ The jaw-dropping 'podracer' scenes from *Star Wars: The Phantom Menace* use computer animation to take the viewer on a dizzying low-altitude flight. When the *Star Wars* series began in 1977, computers were too slow to create such realistic animation effects.

Sound and colour

All early films were silent, and shot in black-and-white. When actors spoke, their words appeared in writing on the screen. Movies with sound – or 'talkies', as they were known – were not really practical until about 1925. Colour came sooner to the cinema. There were crude colour movies by 1906, but 50 years would pass before even half of all films were made in colour.

Animation

Artists began making animated films (cartoons) in 1906. To make their creations come to life, they drew hundreds of similar pictures, with moving objects positioned slightly differently in each one. Photographed and projected in rapid succession, the images danced into action. Computer animation uses a similar method. Animators create the film frame-by-frame. They no longer laboriously draw each picture, though. Instead, they build electronic 'models' of everything that moves. Wrapping the models in realistic textures, and lighting them in a lifelike way, completes the movie illusion.

◀ ▲ Cute cartoon creatures begin their lives on animators' computers in the form of coloured meshes called 'wireframes'. They do not look lifelike, but they are quick and easy to make. Turning them into believable figures, such as Mike Wazowski from *Monsters Inc*, takes longer than the wireframe animation – the movie took more than four years to complete.

▼ Watching a 3-D (three-dimensional) film, the audience reaches out to touch objects that seem to be right in front of them. Special glasses make sure that viewers' eyes see two slightly different pictures. Their brains merge the images to create the illusion of depth.

SUMMARY OF CHAPTER 1: COMMUNICATIONS

Phones to satellites

The mobile phones that make our lives so easy have been around only since the 1970s. Regular telephones began a century earlier, sending voice messages along wires designed to carry the clicks of Morse code. Modern phone calls still travel along copper wires. Over longer distances, speech and data are more likely to travel as bursts of light in fibre-optic cables. International calls also use a network of communications satellites. Like radio stations in orbit about Earth's Equator, these relay calls between dishes on opposite sides of the globe; they carry TV pictures as well.

A geostationary satellite studies a hurricane on Earth

Computers getting connected

Modern communication relies on computers. Although mechanical computers existed in the 19th century, programmable electronic computers began only about 50 years ago. Integrated circuits, invented in the 1960s, made computers small and cheap enough to put on every desk. The internet that linked them together was once a military network for controlling missiles. In the 1990s, it expanded rapidly with the invention of email and the World Wide Web, an easy-to-use, point-and-click interface.

Digital broadcasts

Computers and digital technology power our entertainment, too. Digital broadcasts squeeze far more channels into the limited number of radio and TV wavelengths available. Even movies rely on computers – for animation and special effects and, increasingly, for every part of their production, from camera to screen. However, movies, radio and TV have histories much longer than that of the computer: movies began as moving pictures in 1894; radio first crackled into life about ten years later; and pictures flickered on the first television screens in 1926.

Go further...

Who invented the telephone? This web page compares rival claims:
www.loc.gov/rr/scitech/mysteries/telephone.html

Build your own website and learn how the internet works:
www.webmonkey.com/webmonkey/kids/lessons/index.html

'Marconi calling' is a busy site about the inventor of radio communication:
www.marconicalling.com

Communication: From Hieroglyphs to Hyperlinks
by Richard Platt (Kingfisher, 2004)

Satellite Fever by Mike Painter (Portland Press, 1997)

Fibre-optic telecommunications engineer
Lays and repairs fibre-optic cables and installs equipment linking them to a communications network.

Satellite controller
Keeps satellites operating normally, checking and installing software and monitoring performance.

Application software engineer
Writes software to create programs for computer work (not for systems).

Radio broadcast assistant
Helps with the day-to-day running of a radio station, by researching radio programmes, looking after guests and handling listener feedback.

Find out about TV cameras and animated films at:
The National Museum of Photography, Film and TV, Bradford, West Yorkshire BD1 1NQ, UK
Telephone: +44 (0) 870 7010 200
www.nmpft.org.uk

Learn all about the telephone at:
The Telephone Museum, McConnell Drive, Wolverton, Milton Keynes MK12 5EL, UK
Telephone: +44 (0) 1908 316 222
www.mkheritage.co.uk/TTM

Explore vintage computers at:
Computer History Museum, 1401 N Shoreline Boulevard, Mountain View, California 94043, USA
Telephone: +1 650 810 1010
www.computerhistory.org

CHAPTER 2

Technology in the home

Surging through the wires that wrap our houses, electricity is like an invisible – but essential – servant. It lights and heats our rooms, it keeps our food fresh in the fridge and it takes the work out of unpleasant chores. Electricity powers countless more household inventions that stop us feeling bored or lonely, and it runs the smart and ever-smaller devices that we use to record and remember our lives.

Channelled round the chips of a digital camera, battery power records crystal-clear photographic images. In a camcorder these electric pictures spring into action, forming a video diary of great moments we want to cherish forever. And in video games and portable music players, it is electric power that makes road-racers roar, and songlines soar. So, next time you flip a switch, spare a thought for Thomas Edison, the inventive genius who, with his creation of light bulbs, first brought electricity into the home about 125 years ago.

Coloured X-ray of a low-energy light bulb

◀ Nobody invented electricity. It is a natural form of energy that was not fully understood until the 19th century. Though many scientists studied electricity and helped us use it, Michael Faraday (1791–1867) did more than most. He was the first to show how movement and magnetism could together produce electricity. He made the first dynamo (electricity generator) and the first electric motor.

Electricity and light

Flick a switch, and a light comes on. It is an everyday miracle we take for granted – until there is a power cut. Then, we are in the dark. Without electricity, we cannot heat or clean our homes, cook our food, or watch TV. Power cuts remind us that there is much more to electricity than bulbs and appliances. Each switch connects us to a vast grid of thick cables, and a network of power stations.

The first light bulb

Thomas Edison was just one of many inventors trying to perfect light bulbs. He succeeded in 1879, using a glass bulb emptied of air. The glowing filament inside was made from sewing thread, baked to turn it into black carbon. Edison's bulbs were the first electrical appliances. They replaced flickering candles and gas flames – but only in homes that were connected to electricity supply cables. Edison's company laid cables in the streets and built power stations – his light bulbs would have been useless without a power supply to make them glow.

▶ At night, these shops in Shanghai, China, are brought to to life by electricity.

Power stations and the grid

Today, all developed countries rely on networks of thick cables to carry electricity from power stations to homes, factories and offices. Most power stations generate electricity from fossil fuels – coal, oil or gas. Burning these fuels turns water into steam, which spins huge turbines. These in turn work the dynamos that create electricity.

▲ A satellite view of Earth at night shows who has the power. A pattern of light picks out cities in Europe, North America, south and east Asia. Africa is mostly in darkness. This is because fewer people live there, and those who do cannot afford electricity.

Renewable energy

Saving electricity is important because Earth is running out of the coal, oil and gas we burn in order to make it. And when we burn these fossil fuels, harmful gases are released and they trap heat in our atmosphere. This change in the climate destroys wildlife. It is also melting the world's glaciers, which could raise sea levels and drown our cities. To stop this happening, we must all use less power, and harness new sources of energy, such as the wind, waves, tides and sun.

▶ Wind turbines such as these generate power without using up scarce resources. They do not produce the exhaust gases that trap heat in the atmosphere. Electricity produced without burning fossil fuels is called renewable energy. We can produce it not only from wind, but also from tides and from water dams. Though renewable energy can help stop climate change, we cannot produce enough of it to replace fossil fuels. We must also all use less power.

◀ For many years after the invention of photography, cameras were huge and hard to use. They needed tripods (three-legged stands) to keep them still. This 1877 image shows a park photographer who developed pictures in his handy darkroom cart.

▶ By the late 20th century, cameras were small, light and easy to use. Single-lens reflex cameras such as this one had interchangeable lenses so photographers could magnify distant details – or take pictures in a room as small as a telephone box.

Photography

How can you capture a memory and keep it forever? With a digital camera, it is easy. These compact electronic gadgets are always there when you need them, because they are small enough to slip in your pocket. And when you have frozen a moment that you never want to forget, you can look at it immediately on an LCD (liquid-crystal display). Or, connect the camera to a computer to print or email your snap, or to post it on the web.

The first captured images
Photography was very different when it was invented in 1839 by Frenchman Louis Daguerre (1787–1851). The cameras he used were huge and heavy. Taking each picture took 20 minutes – so he could not record moving subjects. Making the picture visible required dangerous chemicals and a darkened room. The pictures, called daguerrotypes, looked more like mirrors than prints. Photography gradually got easier. Cameras got smaller, and could soon capture moving subjects. With Kodak's introduction of cheap, simple 'box cameras' in 1900, anyone could take pictures.

Digital chips

It was computer chips that made digital photography possible, sweeping away the film and chemicals. Today's digital cameras use dozens of chips. At the camera's heart is a chip that is sensitive to light. Working like digital film, this chip records the image projected onto it from the camera's lens, turning light into computer data. More chips process the data. They use it to show the image on the camera's LCD. Finally, they store it on yet another chip inside the camera's memory card.

▲ X-rays are a form of invisible radiation. Their high energy allows them to pass through solid objects that block light. Captured on film, X-rays can produce a photograph of broken bones — or cracks in pipes.

▲ Connected to a digital camera by a simple cable, a laptop computer can display every picture you have taken today — or fill the screen with a single colourful image.

▼ With digital cameras, it is easier to take clearer pictures, but smart cameras cannot replace photographic skills — especially when attempting tricky, high-speed shots. Professional photographers often use the same equipment as enthusiasts, but their experience and quick reactions enable them to get really great images.

Camcorders

Lights! Camera! Action! Just a few years ago, it was only directors on big-budget Hollywood movies who set the cameras rolling with these words. But today, anyone can be a movie director. Digital camcorders that produce movies good enough to broadcast are small and cheap – and you can buy them in high-street shops. It is easy to edit movies, too, with simple-to-use software that can help you cut out the boring shots, add a soundtrack, and then transfer your masterpiece onto a DVD.

eyepiece

removable battery unit

LCD (liquid-crystal display)

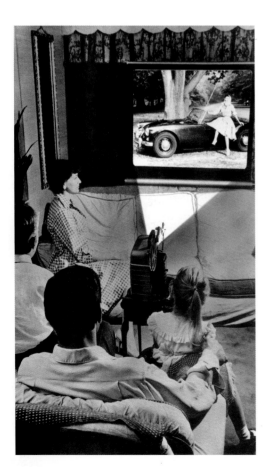

◄ Before video camcorders became popular and cheap, watching home movies meant drawing the curtains, setting up a screen and threading loops of film through a projector.

Film

Home movies began not with video, but with film. Keen enthusiasts used small cameras to film their families as early as 1900. Home movies became really popular in the 1960s with the introduction of Super-8 cameras. They were simple to use, and the film they shot came sealed inside an easy-load cartridge. However, like earlier home movies, Super-8 films were expensive and hard to edit. You could not see what you had shot until you processed the film and projected it.

The arrival of video

Video changed all this: it let you see your movie immediately on a TV set, and you could reuse the tape. The first home video cameras had thick cables to tie together the cameras and recorders. All-in-one camcorders were the idea of Jerome Lemelson (1923–97). The first, the Sony *Betamovie*, appeared in 1982. It was as big as a telephone directory!

microphone

digital videotape

image sensor

lens

▲ Editing a movie at home is now as simple as dragging and dropping icons on a computer screen. Besides changing the order of the shots, you can add special effects, such as fading from one shot to another, and creating animated titles. Mixing in music is simple, too. And once the movie is finished, you can transfer it onto a DVD to show to friends and family.

▲ Although camcorders come in many shapes and sizes, most share the same basic features. A zoom lens at the front focuses a picture on the image sensor. This turns the light into an electronic signal that the camera can process and store on a digital videotape or disc. The eyepiece and LCD show you what you are filming, and a rechargeable battery powers everything.

◄ Video cameras are simple enough for children to use – but adults may need some help!

Digital camcorders

Digital technology made today's compact camcorders possible. By storing images as computer data, they squeeze an hour's video onto a tiny cassette. Because the images are digital, you can store and edit them on your computer, just like any other digital file. Wannabe film-makers have been quick to see the advantages of tiny, cheap camcorders. They have used them to make low-budget movies. Some have had startling success: *The Blair Witch Project* (1999), made for just $40,000 (£23,000), earned its makers more than $100 million (£58 million).

Computer games

J umping and running through grungy cityscapes or battling evil foes, characters in modern computer games are so slick and realistic that they look almost alive. No longer child's play, games are hard to master, and have plots that keep even adults glued to the screen. The games depend on modern computing power for their spectacular effects. Not long ago, when computers were slower and simpler, on-screen characters were simple stick figures and the only sports simulations were crude ping-pong games.

▲ The 1978 arcade game *Space Invaders* had crude graphics, but few could resist shooting down advancing aliens! It was so popular that some Japanese cities ran out of the 100-yen coins that players fed into the machines.

▼ The first home consoles came bundled with a selection of software. Most of it was dull and slow compared to today's games. This boy is playing noughts and crosses in the mid 1970s.

The first computer game
Almost as soon as computers had screens, programmers began writing computer games. The first was the 1962 creation of Stephen Russell (born 1937), a student at the Massachusetts Institute of Technology, USA. In the game, two simple spacecraft (triangles) fired torpedoes (dots) at each other as they orbited a planet (circle). Called *Spacewar*, the game was addictive, but it needed a computer costing the equivalent of six years' wages for a programmer.

Arcade machines
Arcade (coin-operated) games began with table-tennis. Even simpler than *Spacewar*, *Pong* used lines for bats and a square for a ball, but it became hugely popular. The invention of American Nolan Bushnell (born 1943), *Pong* launched the computer-games industry. Home computer-game consoles that plugged into TV sets first appeared in 1972.

▼ Sony's hand-held *PSP* (*PlayStation Portable*) has better graphics than most business computers.

▲ It takes many different skills to create a good computer game. While electronic aids help programmers to create convincing characters, there is still no substitute for an artist's drawing ability.

Hi-tech consoles

Today, the fastest and most exciting computer games run on consoles. Designed for realism and speed, they have the most advanced image-processing chips to create smooth, quickly changing graphics. Linked to other players by cordless controllers, or over the internet, gamers can compete with their best friends – or with strangers they may never meet!

▶ Computer games are not just for youngsters. Adults play them; the games industry makes more money than the movie business; and games heroes often end up in films. Gun-waving characters such as Lara Croft worry parents, but simulation games such as *The Sims* have shown that fast cars, blood and gore are not essential for success.

Music

What kind of music is on the soundtrack to your life? Pop? Hip-hop? R'n'B? Drum and bass? If you have a personal music player such as the iPod, you can listen to whatever you want, wherever you are. And you can pick and choose tracks from online libraries that offer an almost limitless choice of tunes. But access to music was not always this easy and music players were not always small and personal.

Cylinders and discs

For most of the 20th century, the gramophone, invented by Emile Berliner (1851–1925) in 1888, dominated music in the home. This machine was similar to Edison's phonograph (see above, right), but played records rather than cylinders. Today, DJs (disc jockeys) still spin vinyl records on turntables, but most people want a smaller, less fragile way to store music.

◄ In 1877, Thomas Edison invented the phonograph, the first machine that both played and recorded music. A needle moved over a rotating, grooved cylinder, producing music from a large wooden horn.

▲ Sony's *Walkman* was introduced in 1979. It was the first truly pocket-sized personal music player and it had brilliant sound quality. It changed the way people listened to music, and *where* they could listen to it. Its headphones also meant that only *you* heard the music you had chosen.

Mobile music

Transistor radios launched mobile music in the 1950s, but you could not choose what you listened to. It was not until 1963, and the invention of the tape cassette, that music players became truly personal. Even then, they were hardly portable: the clunky tape player was the size of a large book, and there was only one speaker that produced a tinny sound.

Cassette tapes were convenient, but they were technically a step backwards. To cram an hour of music onto each one, the tape had to move slowly through the player, creating a horrible hiss that clever electronics fought hard to reduce.

Digital music

The invention of compact discs (CDs) in 1983 introduced high-quality music that was truly reliable for the first time. CDs stored music as digital data – a series of zeroes and ones – encoded as microscopic pits in the disc's shiny surface and read by a laser beam. CDs sound no better than vinyl played on the best hi-fi systems, but CDs were better at resisting scratches and dust. Within ten years, CD sales overtook vinyl and cassettes. Soon only DJs and hi-fi buffs were spinning the large black records.

▲ Pressed into the surface of a shiny compact disc, tiny pits record the music. A laser beam shines a spot of light onto the disc surface, and when the disc spins, the pits, and the reflective areas in between them, create a flashing code that the CD player reads as digital data. A computer within the player converts the code back into sound.

▶ With its clean, simple design and high-quality sound, the iPod was an instant success when it was introduced in 2001. The iTunes library that Apple created to feed music to iPods changed the music industry, turning downloads from a crime into a profitable business.

Downloading and swapping

CDs did not really change how people bought and listened to music. It took the internet to do that. Music fans were fed up with over-priced albums padded with second-rate tracks. So they began swapping files – illegally – on the internet. A new file format helped. Encoding tracks as MP3s cut their size by nine-tenths. MP3 players, introduced in 1998, moved music away from computers and into listeners' pockets. Shaken by the popularity of 'file-swapping', the music industry finally began selling music online in 2003. Today, the internet is the largest music store in the world, selling millions of tracks and albums.

SUMMARY OF CHAPTER 2: TECHNOLOGY IN THE HOME

Powering up our lives

We depend on electric power. It lights our homes, and often heats them, too. It powers appliances that make our lives more comfortable. Scientists working about 130 years ago devised the basic inventions that brought electricity into the home. They not only created household appliances such as light bulbs, they also had to find ways of making and distributing electricity. While we now cannot manage without electricity, our need for power is causing problems. We must all use less to prevent our planet from overheating.

Recording our memories

The newest modern cameras are like fast, clever computers, storing images and

A racing game on a Sony PSP (PlayStation Portable)

movies as digital files. The first 'still' cameras were invented in France in 1839. They captured images of still objects on polished metal plates. Cameras quickly improved so that they could record moving subjects. Home video cameras are quite a recent invention, first appearing in the mid 1970s. Camcorders, a combination of video cameras and recorders, replaced the Super-8 film cameras, which were until then the favourite way to shoot home movies.

Music and entertainment

Computer games are almost as old as electronic computers. The first ran on colossal and expensive machines found only in laboratories. As computers got smaller and cheaper, arcade games appeared, running on coin-operated consoles. Home computer games followed in the 1970s. Today's games are pocket-sized, but music players are smaller still: some MP3 players are no bigger than a pack of gum. They replaced portable compact-disc players. And the CD players were an advance on cassette-tape players, which – together with transistor radios – started the portable music revolution in the 1950s and 60s.

Go further...

Visit Electricity Online at: http://library.thinkquest.org/28032

Create a colour photograph from two black-and-white pictures: www.pbs.org/wgbh/amex/eastman/sfeature/color.html

Check out the American Museum of the Moving Image: www.movingimage.us/exhibitions/cs98

Play the world's first computer game, *Spacewar*, recreated at: http://lcs.www.media.mit.edu/groups/el/projects/spacewar/

Eyewitness: Music by Neil Ardley (Dorling Kindersley, 2002)

Photographer's assistant
Helps professional photographers in the studio and on location. Work includes setting up equipment and operating lights.

Games developer
Works as part of a team to develop story, sound and visual effects for new electronic games, and writes program code for parts of the game.

Electrical-power engineer
Designs and organizes major electric-power projects, planning power generation and distribution systems.

Digital-music web developer
Helps build interactive websites for digital music stores.

Visit a museum where everything is electric, right down to the boot warmers! The Museum of Electricity The Old Power Station, Bargates, Christchurch, Dorset BH23 1QE, UK Telephone : +44 (0) 1202 480 467 www.scottish-southern.co.uk/museum

Discover the home of Britain's photography pioneer: Fox Talbot Museum, Lacock, Chippenham, Wiltshire SN15 2LG, UK Telephone: +44 (0) 1249 730 459 www.r-cube.co.uk/fox-talbot

Find out about renewable energy at: Centre for Alternative Technology Machynlleth, Powys SY20 9AZ, UK Telephone: +44 (0) 1654 705 950 www.cat.org.uk

CHAPTER 3

Transport

From the frozen wastes of Antarctica to the searing deserts of North Africa, there is hardly anywhere on Earth's surface that people have not explored. Once remote and hard to get to, these places are now within reach of anyone who can afford the ticket – thanks to a bewildering variety of powerful vehicles. Some, such as fast powerboats, are simply improvements on traditional ways of travelling. However, the most exciting of today's super-vehicles are the completely new inventions. Private spacecraft, for example, could soon be opening up near space to wealthy tourists. Transport in all its forms gives us fantastic freedom and enjoyment, but there is a price to pay. Motor vehicles and aircraft choke our atmosphere with their fumes, causing climate change. Unless we invent vehicles that rely less on fossil fuels for power and so produce less pollution, transport will destroy the very places we want to visit.

Cars

We love them. We hate them. But we cannot give them up. Cars are essential to us. They give us the freedom to go anywhere, and to live in remote places. But cars are a huge problem, too. Their exhaust fumes pollute the atmosphere, and may make our world too warm to live in. Today, car manufacturers are racing to build vehicles that are kinder to the environment.

▲ Henry Ford and his son Edsel take a ride in one of his many versions of the Model T motor car in about 1912.

Cheaper cars

Only the very rich could afford the first cars, so in 1900 there were just 11,000 in the whole world (today, there are about 500 million). Factory production of 'motor cars' made them cheap enough for most people and American motor pioneer Henry Ford (1863–1947) was among the first to build cars in large numbers. His factories began making the Ford Model T in 1908. Over the next 20 years, Ford made 15 million of them.

Robot cars

Today's cars have little in common with the Model T except wheels, engine and the driver – and even the driver may soon be unnecessary. Computer scientists are working to make cars that drive themselves. So far, these vehicles are safe only on empty desert roads. But if they could speed through traffic, they could make motorways safer and travel more pleasant.

▲ In 2005, racing to win a $2 million (£1.2 million) prize, 23 robot cars drove themselves 212km through the desert in Nevada, USA. The winning car, 'Stanley' (above, left), finished in less than seven hours. Laser range-finders, video cameras and six computers kept Stanley on course.

◄ Electric cars that drivers charge up at filling stations are no solution for climate change. Though the cars themselves do not cause pollution, power stations must burn fossil fuels to generate the electricity that tops up their batteries. 'Hybrid' cars such as the Toyota *Prius* are better: they combine petrol and electric motors to reduce fuel use. However, the only long-term solution is less driving, and more public transport.

'Greener' cars

When cars first appeared, people thought they would cure pollution, not cause it. Before German engineer Gottlieb Daimler (1834–1900) invented petrol engines in 1884, transport was powered by horses. And horse dung was smelly and hard to clear from streets! Today, car manufacturers are aware of the harmful gases that petrol engines produce and are looking for alternative power sources, such as hydrogen, electricity and solar energy.

▼ Scientists use crash-test dummies to study the forces exerted on people during car crashes.

Controlling traffic

As cars multiplied, inventors looked for ways to keep traffic moving safely. Electric traffic lights began in 1914 in the American city of Cleveland. They had only two colours – red and green – and a buzzer, which sounded to warn when the lights were about to change. Reflective road studs, to separate lanes of traffic, were the 1933 invention of English road repairer Percy Shaw. The eyes of a cat shining in his headlights inspired the invention – and gave it its familiar nickname: 'cat's eyes'.

Trains

▲ George Stephenson's *Rocket* famously won an 1829 competition to choose a locomotive for a railway linking Liverpool and Manchester in the UK.

Floating above its track as if it weighed nothing, the world's most advanced train can speed along at four times the speed of a car. Few modern trains can match the Chinese magnetic levitation (Maglev) system for speed and efficiency, but even ordinary trains share many of its advantages. Compared to cars, railways are safer and less polluting – and they do not suffer from traffic jams. No wonder trains remain a popular form of transport two centuries after their invention.

The first trains

Miners in Germany pushed carts that ran on rails as early as 1519. And, by 1712, the first steam engines were also used in mines, to pump out water. In 1803, British engineer Richard Trevithick (1771–1833) was the first to combine steam power and rails to make a steam-powered locomotive. George Stephenson (1781–1848) later improved on Trevithick's invention and, by 1850, railway lines linked many large towns in the UK and abroad.

New locomotives

Steam powered most trains until 1913, when diesel locomotives began to haul trucks and carriages. The new diesel engines burned oil to power pistons directly – rather than to make steam, which in turn pushed the pistons. This meant that a diesel loco used half as much fuel as a steam locomotive pulling a similar train. Diesel engines still power many of the world's trains, except on the busiest lines.

▲ Freight trains (trains that transport goods), such as this one in Jordan, can move enormous loads over very long distances. Rail transport, compared to road transport, is safer, cheaper and less harmful to the environment – a typical freight train can carry 50 lorry loads over the same route.

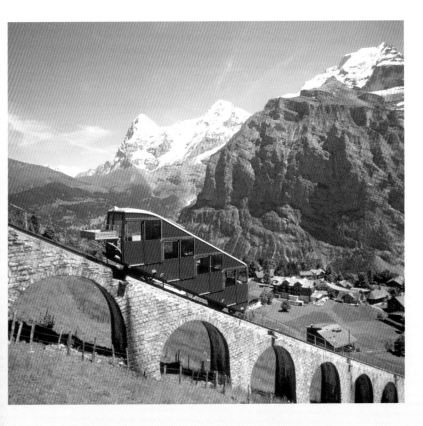

Electric power

The most efficient way of powering trains is with electricity. However, supplying power through an extra rail or an overhead wire makes electric railway lines expensive to build. The first electric trains transported passengers in city areas, and underground (where smoke from steam locomotives caused problems). Today, electricity powers the most advanced rail networks, including the high-speed lines on which trains travel faster than 200km/h.

Maglev trains

Electricity powers and lifts Maglev trains. Electromagnets in the track push upwards against magnets in the train, lifting it off the ground. More electromagnets push the carriages forward. As the train does not touch anything, only friction with the air slows it down. Maglev trains do not need wheels at high speeds, but some of them do use wheels when travelling slowly – and in case the power fails. Existing Maglev trains whizz along at up to 430km/h – future trains may go as fast as jet aircraft.

▲ 'Funicular' trains operate on steep slopes. They are hauled up on a cable pulled by an engine at the top of the hill. Instead of this cable, some mountain railways have a third, toothed rail (between the two normal rails) that cog-wheels on the train grip on to.

▼ The Shanghai Maglev train in China floats one centimetre above its tracks.

Sea vehicles

Like a watery highway, the oceans link the continents with a vast, free transport route. Immense cargo ships slowly carry goods around the world, while hovercraft and hydrofoils ferry passengers and vehicles at much faster speeds, skimming above the waves. Though we have been sailing the ocean's surface for more than 6,000 years, we began journeys beneath it less than two centuries ago. Today, submarines can withstand the crushing pressure, cold and constant darkness to reach the deepest ocean floor.

▲ This old sketch shows one of the first ever submarines. It was built by Dutch inventor Cornelius Drebbel (1572–1633) in the 1620s. Powered by oars, the sub travelled up London's River Thames, in the UK, about 4m underwater. The crew breathed air through tubes that reached up to the surface.

▶ The smallest submarines, or submersibles, do not even need crews: controlled from afar they can go deeper without risking lives.

How submarines work

Before deep-sea submarines were possible, inventors had to solve problems of pressure, power, air supply and waterproofing. Early subs had weak hulls made of greased leather so they could not dive deep. However, modern submarines are strong enough to resist the crushing weight of the water above. Instead of oars, they are powered by motors that do not need air to work. Crafts carry their own air supply, and to surface or dive the crews fill 'ballast tanks' with either air or seawater to change the submarines' weight.

War under the waves

Most submarines are used for warfare. Under the waves, submarines are invisible, and can creep up on enemy shipping undetected. Ordinary submarines have to surface regularly to stock up on air for the crew to breathe, and to recharge their batteries. Nuclear submarines do not have these problems. Their power plants need no air to work, and air for breathing is recycled. A nuclear sub could sail seven times around the world before its power ran out.

◄ On the surface, a mothership steers a tiny, uncrewed submersible. A flexible tether links the two vessels. The tether combines data and power cables. The data cable enables scientists on the mothership to control the sub's thrusters, which drive it forwards. It also allows them to watch pictures from on-board video cameras.

On the surface

Hovercraft, invented in 1952 by Christopher Cockerell (1910–99), float on a cushion of air. They work as well on mud, ice and quicksand as they do on the sea. Hydrofoils reduce the friction that slows them down by rising out of the water. An undersea 'wing' raises the hull, just as a regular wing lifts a plane into the air.

▲ Modern ocean liners such as the *Queen Mary 2* are like luxurious floating cities. With space for more than 2,600 passengers, the ship has a cinema and a virtual golf course. Its power plant could provide enough electricity to light 200,000 homes.

▼ A hovercraft's ability to move freely on almost any surface makes it a useful vehicle where land meets water. This hovercraft is used for ocean rescue off the UK's northwest coast. It can cross shallow water and mud that would stop an ordinary lifeboat.

Aviation

At a windy airport, a huge aircraft powers down the runway and, with a deafening roar, is blasted into the air by its four huge engines. The Airbus A380 is a 'superjumbo' and the world's largest passenger airliner, larger even than the Boeing 747, which ruled the skies for 35 years. Powerful jet aircraft make travel so safe, quick and easy that we forget just how amazing it is to fly. Yet it is hardly more than a century since the Wright brothers, Orville and Wilbur, invented aviation.

▲ Two American bicycle engineers from Dayton, Ohio, USA, were the first to build a working aircraft. A week before Christmas 1903, Orville (1871–1948) and Wilbur (1867–1912) Wright powered up the engine on *Flyer*, and Orville took off from the sand at Kill Devil Hill on North Carolina's windy coast. Their longest flight that day lasted just 59 seconds, but it earned them a place in history. This picture shows an improved Wright aircraft flying over Kill Devil Hill in 1911.

Giants of the air
It is not easy to grasp the sheer scale of an airliner. At 73m, the A380 is longer than eight buses. It can move the population of a large village 15,000km without landing to refuel. But the A380 is a toy compared to the biggest of the world's aircraft. The airships that ferried passengers across the Atlantic Ocean in the 1930s were three times as long. Their passenger cabins hung beneath gigantic balloons, held in place by aluminium frames.

▲ Airships seemed like the future of aviation in the 1930s — until the huge *Hindenburg* burst into flames at Lakehurst, New Jersey, USA, in 1937. After the accident, few travellers dared fly in a balloon.

▲ Built to show off the engineering skills of the UK and France, *Concorde* flew the super-rich across the Atlantic Ocean for 27 years. Because of the air and noise pollution that supersonic airliners cause, there will probably never be another aircraft like it.

Faster and higher

No aircraft is ever fast enough for impatient passengers. So in the 1950s, aviation companies began designing planes to fly faster than the speed of sound. *Concorde*, built jointly by the UK and France, first flew passengers in 1976. Travelling at 2,170km/h (about twice the speed of sound), it took just 3.5 hours to cross the Atlantic Ocean from Paris or London to New York, USA. Unfortunately, at full speed the aircraft was too noisy to fly over areas where people lived, which is one of the reasons why the aircraft never made any money.

◄ The newest warplanes are invisible weapons. Stealth technology hides them from radar – the radio detection system used to aim anti-aircraft defences. To reduce its radar reflection, this Lockheed F-117A Nighthawk has sharp angles and is covered in radar-absorbing paint. Unfortunately, the paint runs off in the rain, so the F-117A operates only on fine days.

▼ The round radar dome above the rotor of this AH-64 Apache helicopter allows the pilot to 'look over' a building or hill-top and fire deadly weapons while hovering out of sight.

Flying windmills

An ordinary aircraft needs a long runway to pick up speed, because it relies on air rushing quickly over its wings to lift it. However, a helicopter spins its wings to get the rush of air it needs to fly – so it can take off from small spaces. Italian artist and inventor Leonardo da Vinci sketched a helicopter in the 15th century, but it took until the 20th century for the first 'chopper' to fly – built by French bicycle engineer Paul Cornu in 1907. Modern helicopters do a variety of jobs that would be impossible for fixed-wing aircraft. They can land on oil-rigs, ships and hospital roofs; they can ferry rock stars to gigs; and they can transport troops and equipment in and out of remote war zones.

Space travel

Travelling into space and floating weightlessly, high above Earth once seemed like a ridiculous dream, but for astronauts on the Space Shuttle, it has become almost routine. Though just seven lucky astronauts fly in each Shuttle, space travel may soon become the newest white-knuckle ride. If private space vehicles like *SpaceShipOne* succeed, space tourism will be within reach of anyone who can afford a ticket.

▲ The first space passenger vehicle was the Russian *Vostok 1* capsule launched in 1961. Cosmonaut (space pilot) Yuri Gagarin (1934–68) was really just cargo — he had no control over the course his capsule took. *Vostok 1* circled Earth once while Gagarin looked out of a porthole: '…Earth is bluish,' he commented.

▼ The Space Shuttle *Discovery* is prepared for launch at the Kennedy Space Centre, USA, in June 2005. The Shuttle rides piggy-back on two solid fuel rocket boosters and a giant tank (orange in this picture) that fuels the Shuttle's own rocket engines.

The X Prize

The $10-million (£6-million) X Prize was set up to encourage private space flight. To win it, a space vehicle had to fly into space (100km above Earth) with a crew of three, return safely and then repeat the journey within a fortnight. A small US company won the prize in October 2004 with *SpaceShipOne*. A lightweight jet aircraft, *White Knight*, carried the craft up to 15.2km before *SpaceShipOne*'s rocket engine fired and blasted it to the edge of space.

◀ *SpaceShipOne* hangs beneath its jet aircraft mothership *White Knight*. The two aircraft have identical cockpits, but *SpaceShipOne* has a rocket motor that powers it into space.

Reusable spacecraft

Less than one month after Yuri Gagarin became the first person in space, NASA (the USA's National Aeronautics and Space Administration) launched its own space vehicle, *Freedom 7*. Its pilot, Alan Shepard (1923–98), experienced weightlessness for five minutes before his capsule splashed safely into the Atlantic Ocean.

In 1981, 20 years after Gagarin's space flight, NASA launched the first Space Shuttle, *Columbia*. The Shuttle was designed to be reused. When friction with the air heats an ordinary spacecraft on its return to Earth, its outer layer burns up. The Shuttle, however, resisted the heat with a covering of ceramic tiles. The Shuttle was partly successful, but there have been deadly accidents – in 2003, for example, *Columbia* exploded on its return to Earth.

Sailing through space

Future space probes may not need rocket fuel: instead they could be blown along with a sail. Space is a vacuum: there is no air and, therefore, no wind. However, light from the Sun creates a tiny pressure on everything it strikes. By unfolding a giant sail, a spacecraft could use this 'radiation pressure' to power it across huge distances. Scientists predict that the craft's speed could reach 60km per second, but they have yet to test their ideas. The first space sailing ship crashed during its launch in 2005.

▶ The pressure from sunlight that pushes a solar sail along is tiny: the equivalent to 15g in weight pushing on an area the size of a football pitch. So the sail has to be huge, as this example from NASA shows. Even with a giant sail, spacecraft powered by radiation pressure would gather speed very slowly.

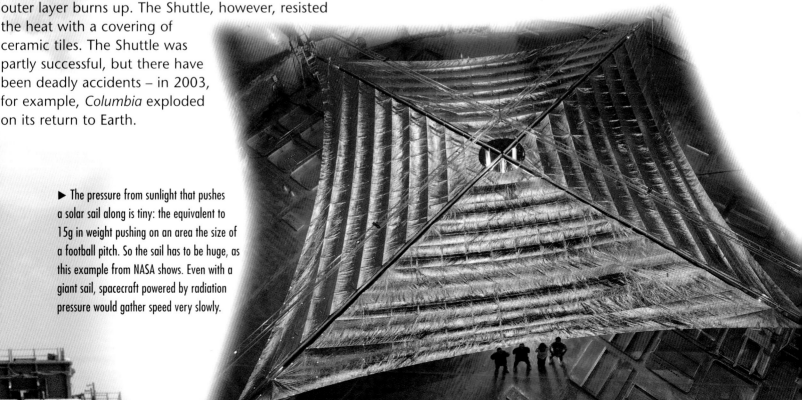

SUMMARY OF CHAPTER 3: TRANSPORT

On road and rail

The invention of petrol engines in the late 19th century made cars possible and, within just 40 years, they had almost replaced horse transport. Though cars give travellers great freedom, their exhaust fumes damage our planet's climate. Today, car makers are looking for alternative fuels, such as electricity, to limit the harm. Rail transport is kinder to the environment, and frees travellers from the headache of traffic jams. Invented nearly a century before cars, railway locomotives were at first powered by steam. Diesel and electric motors

replaced steam in the 20th century. Today, trains are the quickest form of land transport. The most modern need no wheels, and are nearly as fast as aircraft.

An electric car recharges its batteries

Ships, submarines and hydrofoils

Transport at sea is slow but efficient: ships carry huge cargoes at low cost. Their basic shape has hardly changed since the first craft sailed the oceans 6,000 years ago, but today the source of a ship's power is an oil-fired engine, not a sail. Special kinds of ship have made sea transport more versatile. Submarines lurk below the waves to make war or explore ocean depths; and hydrofoils skim just above the surface.

Air and space travel

Soaring high in the atmosphere – and above it – planes and spacecraft are the fastest way of getting around. They are the newest kind of transport, too – nobody flew until 1903. Today, flight is routine, with huge aircraft moving holiday-makers around the world at low cost. Space travel began in only 1961, and is still a dangerous adventure. New space-planes aim to give wealthy tourists a taste of travel beyond the atmosphere. Journeys to other planets – perhaps with beams of light for power – remain a distant dream.

Go further...

Find out how we will get about in years to come at Future Transport:
http://library.thinkquest.org/04oct/01249

Discover fuel cells powered by hydrogen gas: could they be the power source for cars of the future?
www.pbs.org/wgbh/nova/sciencenow/3210/01.html

Enjoy a colourful look at the history of air transport:
www.century-of-flight.freeola.com

The World of Flight by Ian Graham (Kingfisher, 2006)

Eyewitness: Boat by Eric Kentley (Dorling Kindersley, 2000)

Automotive engineer
Member of a large team that designs, develops and tests new vehicles.

Train driver
Operates trains, checks fuel on non-electric locomotives, and performs minor maintenance tasks.

Naval architect
Designs new ships and ocean-going equipment, and organizes their manufacture.

Space-vehicle engineer
Develops ideas for new space vehicles, and cooperates with other engineers to design and build the most practical craft.

Visit an aerospace museum: Smithsonian National Air and Space Museum, Independence Avenue at 4th Street, SW, Washington DC 20560, USA
Telephone: +1 202 633 1000
www.nasm.si.edu

Learn all about railways at: Britain's National Railway Museum Leeman Road, York YO26 4XJ, UK
Telephone: +44 (0) 1904 621 261
www.nrm.org.uk

Discover London's transport at: London Transport Museum, Covent Garden, London WC2E 7BB, UK
Telephone: +44 (0) 20 7565 7299
www.ltmuseum.co.uk
(opening spring 2007)

CHAPTER 4

New technology

Inventions affect our lives in many unexpected and unseen ways, both big and small. Behind the doors of enormous factories, for example, technology has transformed the way things are made, with robots building everything from cars to TV sets. Inventors have been at work on a minute scale as well. In medicine, researchers operate at the level of a single cell to create clones (identical copies of plants and animals). They snip and join up tiny strands of DNA – the rope-like molecule that controls everything about us.

Pharmaceutical researchers have made us healthier, with drugs and jabs to prolong our lives. Another new branch of technology deals with ever-smaller devices. Scarcely bigger than dust, nanomachines are too small to see without a microscope. In the future, they could perform all kinds of amazing services, and even build themselves, atom by atom.

Coloured X-ray image of a microscope

Robotics

Imagine a worker who can do a complicated job 24 hours a day, without sleep, food or breaks. Or who can withstand deadly radiation to make repairs inside a damaged nuclear power plant. Such workers do not exist, but a robot could easily do these jobs. Most robots work in factories, assembling cars and electronic equipment. A few do dangerous jobs such as making bombs safe or exploring space. And domestic robots can clean our floors and mow our lawns.

▲ This automaton was built about 1875 and was called *Psycho*. A form of after-dinner entertainment, it attempted to read the minds of its wealthy audience. Most of these mechanical toys in the 18th and 19th centuries mimicked humans or animals.

▼ Factory robots like these automatic welders have replaced human workers on many dull and dangerous tasks. The success of robots led experts to predict that future factories would not need lighting or heating, because their workers would all be machines. However, this has not happened – robots are still not reliable enough to work on their own, and nobody has yet made a robot that can repair robots!

From toy to worker

Robots began as mechanical toys in the 18th century, built to amuse wealthy people. Very simple systems for controlling machines were invented about the same time. Robots were called 'automata' or 'androids' until 1920 when Czech author Karel Capek (1890–1938) wrote about mechanical workers in his play *R.U.R.* He named them after a Czech word *robota*, meaning 'hard, boring work'. Real robots that could be programmed to perform different tasks were not practical until computers were available to control them in the 1960s.

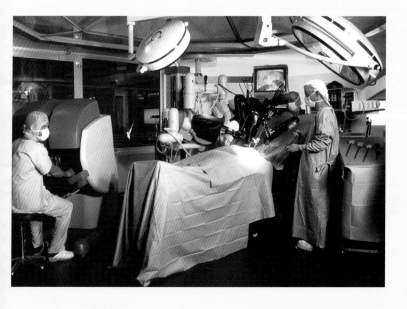

To operate using the da Vinci surgery robot, a surgeon sitting at a console (on the left of this picture) looks into twin eyepieces like a pair of binoculars. These show a three-dimensional image produced by a pair of cameras positioned right inside the patient's body. By moving handles inside the console, the surgeon controls instruments next to the cameras, to grab, move or cut tissue.

Automatic surgery

Letting a robot loose with a scalpel may not sound like a good idea, but growing numbers of robots work in operating theatres. Under the control of a surgeon on the other side of the room, robot arms grip and cut the patient's flesh. Tiny cameras give the surgeon a close-up view in three dimensions. Robot surgery has many advantages: robots' hands can reach through tiny holes, so scars are smaller; and they are absolutely steady, making cuts more precise.

Industrial robots

Putting together cars or computers is dull, hard work, and single-arm robots have replaced humans in many factories. Robots can lift, weld and spray-paint cars faster and better than people can. To program them, real workers first move the arms, 'teaching' the robot what to do. The robot can then repeat exactly the same action a million times. Cameras give robots vision, so that they can identify parts to be assembled.

▼ Honda's *Asimo* is one of the first android (human-like) robots that can mimic human movements such as walking up stairs. Android robots are being developed by car manufacturers to help around the home or office. Currently, the most successful cleaning robot is probably the disc-shaped *Roomba*, which vacuums floors while its owners are out. 'Social robots', disguised as dogs or dinosaurs, are intelligent toys that are strictly for entertainment.

Nanotechnology

Think of the smallest speck of dust you can see. Now picture something 100,000 times smaller. Particles this size are the building blocks for one of the newest, smallest ways of making things: nanotechnology. In the distant future, nanotechnology could create machines that assemble themselves from individual atoms – the smallest particles that make up everything in our world.

▲ Nanotechnology is already in action, in some very useful – if undramatic – ways. By using much tinier particles in industry, highly durable and stain-resistant fabrics can be produced, as well as super filters that remove germs from water, and clear skin creams to protect against sunburn.

▲ Visible under a microscope, microcogs work together to form a microgear mechanism. These mechanisms are used in everything from inkjet printer cartridges to disposable blood-pressure monitors.

▼ Carbon nanotubes, shown here magnified some six million times, have peculiar properties. Injected into the cells of living things, they head straight for the nucleus – the vital centre that controls growth and reproduction. Researchers believe that they will soon be able to use this ability to target drugs at the part of the cell where they will do the most good.

Tiny gears

Strictly speaking, nanotechnology describes devices about one millionth of a millimetre in size. However, the word is often used to cover larger inventions such as MEMS (microelectromechanical systems). Though they are not strictly on a nano scale, you still need a powerful magnifier to see them clearly. MEMS are made just like computer chips, by depositing or etching patterns onto a wafer of silicon. There is a MEMS device in every new car. It triggers the safety airbag in a crash. Just as important, it ensures that the airbag does not open when the driver simply brakes hard.

Carbon nanotubes

What do a pencil mark and a diamond have in common? Quite a lot – both are forms of carbon. Carbon can also exist in a third, recently discovered form, as narrow tubes (nanotubes) or tiny balls (buckyballs). Nanotubes are 50,000 times narrower than a human hair, but may be several centimetres long. Their shape and structure give them immense strength, and unusual electrical properties. A rope made of carbon nanotubes could hoist satellites into space, and they are already being used to make electric motors more reliable. One day, they may help pharmacists to ferry drugs only to diseased cells.

◄ In this imaginative computer image, nanorobots swarm on a brain cell, preparing to inject it with a healing drug. Before such ideas can become reality, scientists must find ways to make and control these tiny devices.

The molecular factory

Scientists already use atomic-force microscopes to arrange atoms one by one. With this technique, they could perhaps build 'nanomachines' small enough to operate inside a living cell – but it would take a very long time. To speed up the process, they aim to create a device that can copy itself, over and over again. Nanotechnology fans predict that the tiny devices will perform surgery from inside our bodies, swimming in arteries to bust heart-stopping blood clots.

At the moment, such ideas are pure science fiction, not fact.

Genetic engineering

Inside your body's cells is a biological code describing you, and only you, in the tiniest detail. Called deoxyribonucleic acid – DNA for short – it is shaped like a 2m-long coiled rope. All living things rely on DNA to pass on information, in the form of genes, from parent to child. By decoding DNA for plants, humans and other animals, scientists have invented a powerful tool. With genetic engineering, we might make crops grow on waste land, or cure the world's most feared diseases.

▼ By moving genes from glowing jellyfish into mice, scientists have bred mice that glow when they are lit up by a beam of ultraviolet, which is not normally visible to the naked eye. These transgenic mice are not novelty pets – the research has a serious purpose. By making cancer cells glow in the same way, doctors could trace – and stop – their deadly progress around the body.

Cracking the code
The coiled-rope shape of DNA was the 1953 discovery of James Watson (born 1928) and Francis Crick (1916–2004). Soon after their breakthrough, scientists began to sequence (decode) DNA to find its structure. Understanding the 'genetic code' of living things enables us to change them. For example, by moving genes from Arctic fish to tomatoes, scientists hoped to create a frost-resistant crop. They failed, but other, similar 'genetic modifications' (GMs) have worked, making plants that resist disease, or taste better.

▼ The curling, rope-like strand of DNA stores biological information as a sequence of chemicals called 'bases'. There are four kinds, and their order is different in each individual – except for identical twins and clones.

Making identical twins

By taking the part of a cell containing DNA – the nucleus – and implanting it into a developing cell that lacks a nucleus, scientists can create copies of plants and animals. This method, called cloning, produced identical frogs in the 1950s. Successful cloning of mammals began in 1984. Scientists hope to make identical twins of the very best farm animals, to provide more and better milk, meat or wool.

▶ In the first stage of the cloning process, researchers remove the DNA from a sheep egg cell (centre). Suction holds the cell firmly against the tube on the left. The sharp glass tube on the right will puncture the cell's outer wall and suck out the nucleus that contains the DNA.

egg cell

nucleus

◀ In 1996, scientists at Scotland's Roslin Institute, in the UK, were the first to produce clones from cells taken from an adult mammal. The result was Dolly the sheep, shown here on the right. Clones such as Dolly could one day be used as living 'drug factories', producing disease-fighting proteins in their milk.

◀ Big chemical companies want farmers to grow genetically modified crops, such as this GM oilseed rape, because it can resist the weedkiller the companies also sell. However, extended use of weedkiller can cause plants to become resistant to it. If this resistance spreads to a weed called charlock, oilseed rape's wild relative, the charlock would spread quickly and be very difficult to control.

Should we do it?

Not everyone agrees that tinkering with DNA is a good thing. Weedkiller-proof, genetically modified (GM) crops, for example, have encouraged farmers to spray their fields more often, killing wildlife. Crops may also cross (breed with) weeds, creating 'super-weeds' that no spray can kill. Critics oppose cloning because they believe it will lead to cloned humans. They fear that by combining genetic modification with cloning, scientists might create 'designer babies', with just the qualities parents want.

Medical technology

A British baby born in 1900 could expect to die 47 years later; a child born today will live – on average – to be 77. Why do we live so much longer now? Improvements in medicine are the most important reason. In one single century, researchers have found vaccines to protect us against many deadly diseases and they have discovered new kinds of drugs to prevent infection. New medical technology enables us to restart a failing heart, or spot cancer deep inside the brain.

▶ Traditional Chinese herbal remedies can help heal diseases that 'modern' medicine cannot. The Chinese cures contain dozens of chemicals, some that work only when combined. Researchers hope to identify which are the healing chemicals, so that they can make cures more effective and reduce harmful side-effects.

Moulds and medicines

The pharmaceutical (drugs) industry today uses genetic engineering (see pages 54–55) to tailor treatments to each patient. This life-saving business relies on constant research by observant scientists. In 1928, one of them, Alexander Fleming (1881–1955), discovered penicillin, the first antibiotic. Since then antibiotics have saved millions of lives by stopping infection.

▶ Penicillin grows in a laboratory dish

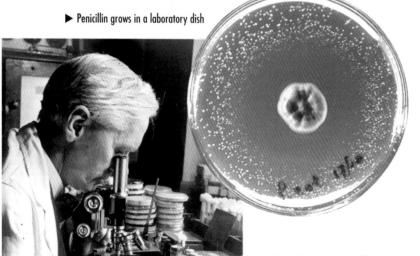

▲ When Alexander Fleming was working in his laboratory in 1928, he noticed that some mould on one of his dishes was killing the germs around it. When purified, this mould became penicillin.

Medical imaging

The discovery of X-rays in 1895, by German physicist Wilhelm Röntgen (1845–1923), greatly aided the medical profession. X-rays gave a good view of hard parts of the body, especially bones, but the invention of computers made them much more useful. Computed tomography (CT) scanners, invented in 1972, formed X-ray images of narrow sections of the body, creating a 3-D picture that showed the soft tissues clearly.

▶ Positron emission tomography (PET), developed in 1974, and magnetic resonance imaging (MRI) scanners, developed in 1977, further improved internal images of the human body. Here (right) an MRI scanner produces cross-section images of a patient's brain.

Jabs for protection

One needle jab can give years of immunity (protection) against disease. This technique of vaccination, discovered in the 18th century, relies on infecting patients with a vaccine – a weakened form of a disease. The world's first vaccination gave immunity from smallpox. Today, there are vaccines against diseases such as measles and polio, but the search is still on for a vaccine against HIV (human immunodeficiency virus), which causes AIDS.

Looking after the developing world

Medicines began as herbal cures. Even today, one-quarter of all drugs comes from plants. People in wealthy nations benefit from both chemical and plant-based medicines, whereas many people who live in poorer parts of the world have access only to traditional medicines. Each year, $4,000 (£2,300) is spent on one American person's healthcare, but only $20 (£11.50) is spent on an African's. Fortunately, a few charities are trying to change this. Business tycoon Bill Gates (born 1955), chairman of the world-famous Microsoft Corporation, is investing money in the search for a cure for malaria, a deadly disease that mainly affects poor countries.

▲ A woman in Malaysian Borneo picks a plant that local people use to relieve pain and to treat skin disease. People who live in rainforest regions all over the world use plants to treat their illnesses. Drug researchers try to tap into this knowledge so that the wider world can benefit.

SUMMARY OF CHAPTER 4: NEW TECHNOLOGY

Obedient machines

Robots began in the 18th century as amusing toys. Today, robots that perform useful jobs surround us. In the home, they wash dishes or vacuum the floor. In industry, robots build and paint cars, and assemble electronic parts. And in war zones or nuclear power plants, robots work in conditions too dangerous for humans. Almost all robots do just one job, and do it very well. Android robots that can do everything for us remain a laboratory dream.

An android robot sophisticated enough to walk up stairs

Small is beautiful

A tiny revolution is transforming industry. Nanotechnology is engineering on a microscopic scale. Scientists are already using it to create ultra-fine coatings, powders and filters, extra-strong materials, and miniature mechanical devices. Some believe that in the distant future nanotechnology will allow us to build things atom-by-atom, assembling robots that are too small to see. They hope that these minute machines will even learn to assemble themselves.

Genetically better?

By decoding our DNA – the 'blueprint' for all human life – scientists have found a new and powerful way of promoting health and conquering disease. Genetic techniques are the latest of many medical breakthroughs that have helped us to live longer. These include medical imaging such as X-rays and CT scans, vaccinations, and powerful drugs made from moulds and plants. The people of wealthy nations have benefited more by these advances than those in the developing world.

Growing knowledge of the genes of animals and plants has allowed researchers to create genetically modified, 'designer' species. However, there is bitter opposition to this work, and to the cloning of animals.

Go further...

Learn to guide a robot rover at: www.thetech.org/robotics

Visit a virtual exhibition about nanotechnology from London's Science Museum, and play the NanoLand game: www.sciencemuseum.org.uk/antenna/nano

Become a DNA detective at this genetic site from the American Museum of Natural History: www.ology.amnh.org/genetics

Genetic Engineering: The Facts by Sally Morgan (Evans Brothers, 2001)

Eyewitness: Robot by Roger Bridgman (Dorling Kindersley, 2004)

Robotics engineer
Designs, builds, programs and services robots for use in industry.

Plant geneticist
Breeds plants to produce varieties that give bigger or better crops, or that grow in less-than-ideal conditions of soil or climate.

Medical-imaging technician
Develops software to process data from MRI scanners, producing clearer images that make diagnosis of disease quicker and more certain.

Nanowire synthesis researcher
Investigates nanowires – ultra-thin wires that could help build the next generation of computers.

Learn about surgery in the past – no anaesthetic! The Old Operating Theatre Museum, 9a St Thomas's Street, London SE1 9RY, UK Telephone: +44 (0) 20 7188 2679 www.thegarret.org.uk/oot.htm

Visit an exhibition about genetics at: The Science Museum, Exhibition Road, London SW7 2DD, UK Telephone: +44 (0) 870 870 4868 www.sciencemuseum.org.uk/on-line/wellcome-wing/index.asp

Explore creativity, discovery and invention at: Royal Museum, Chambers Street, Edinburgh EH1 1JF, Scotland, UK Telephone: +44 (0) 131 247 4422 www.nms.ac.uk/royal/home

Glossary

aerial
Device that receives or transmits a radio signal.

animation
Making a movie from drawings or computer pictures that are different for each frame of the film, creating an illusion of movement.

antenna
See aerial.

antibiotic
Medical drug that stops infections caused by bacteria.

atmosphere
Mixture of gases that surround Earth, making life possible.

atom
The smallest particle of the matter from which everything is made.

atomic-force microscope
Powerful microscope that forms images by measuring the attraction between the subject and a probe at its tip.

audio
To do with sound.

automatic
Happening without any action by people.

ballast tank
Tank that can be filled with air or water to change the weight of a craft.

CAD
Short for computer-aided design.

carbon
An element (basic substance) that exists in several forms: graphite, diamond and nanotubes or buckyballs.

CD
Short for compact disc, a disc that stores information or music in the form of digital data.

circuit
Electrical device made up of parts such as transistors and connecting wires.

communications satellite
A satellite in orbit above Earth that passes on communications signals.

computer chip
A miniaturized circuit for processing data inside a computer.

console
A control panel for a computer, a games device or other machine.

DAB
Short for digital audio broadcasting.

An 'antenna farm'
in Arizona, USA

data
Information, usually stored in a form that computers can understand.

diesel
Kind of engine that makes fuel explode by 'squeezing' it.

digital
Using data in the form of a string of on/off (one/zero) signals – rather than a continuous flow.

DNA
Short for deoxyribonucleic acid: the rope-like molecule that stores information about the shape and structure of living things.

DVD
Short for digital versatile disc, a disc that stores movies.

dynamo
A device that turns movement into electricity.

electric current
Form of energy, flowing in a circuit to power useful devices, or to operate a computer.

electronics
Use of electricity for communications or computing.

filament
Thin strand inside a light bulb that glows when heated by electricity.

friction
The sticky force that stops objects sliding when pressed together.

graphics
Pictures, especially those that make information visible.

hardware
The machinery of a computer – rather than software programs.

hi-fi
Short for high-fidelity (good quality) in recorded sound and music.

HTML
Short for Hypertext Markup Language, the code used to write web pages.

hydrogen
A very light gas that burns with explosive power.

image-processing chip
Part of a computer or games device that draws images on a screen.

integrated circuit
Miniature electronic part that contains many transistors and other devices, on a chip of silicon.

interface
The controls and display of a computer or game.

LCD
Short for liquid-crystal display – the flat screen of a computer, a camera and many other devices.

lens
Shaped piece of glass that gathers rays of light to form sharp pictures.

locomotive
The front part of a train, containing an engine, that pulls the carriages or trucks behind.

microprocessor
Chip that does most of the work in a computer.

A rusting locomotive no longer in service

microwave
Invisible form of energy, similar to light, used for cooking and communications.

molecule
Tiny group of similar or mixed atoms that cannot be separated without changing their qualities.

Morse code
Code of long and short pulses used to spell out the alphabet.

MP3
Method of storing music files and greatly reducing their size – also a name for the files themselves.

nano-
Part-word that divides by one billion the measurement unit that follows it.

nuclear
Based on the splitting of atoms to release great power.

online
Available from a computer network, especially the internet.

optical fibre
Thin glass thread that carries data in the form of light.

pharmaceutical
To do with medical drugs.

piston
Metal block that slides to-and-fro in an engine, driven by steam or fuel.

quantum
To do with the fixed amounts of energy that atoms can possess.

radiation
Energy, such as light or microwaves, spreading as waves, particles or rays.

radio
Form of invisible radiation commonly used for communication.

radio telescope
Telescope that studies the stars by looking at the radio waves they give off.

silicon
Chemical substance, commonly found in sand, that is purified and used for making computer chips.

software
The complex instructions that make a computer work.

stereo
Giving the illusion of depth, in a picture or sound.

telegraphy
Way of communicating using pulses of electricity in Morse code.

transistor
Miniature electronic switch or amplifying part.

transistor radio
A miniature radio that works using transistors.

transmitter
Device that sends out a communication signal.

ultraviolet
Invisible radiation, given off by the Sun and by special lamps, that has more energy than visible light but less than X-rays.

A silicon chip

vaccine
Weakened form of a disease that when absorbed by the body provides protection against the disease itself.

vacuum
Space containing no air or any other substance.

valve
Device that allows a flow in one direction only.

VCR
Short for video cassette recorder.

video
Picture – especially a TV picture.

wavelength
Single channel of communication; or gap between the highest levels in a wave.

web
Short for World Wide Web, the simple system of pages and clickable links that makes the internet easy to use.

Index

Acknowledgements

The publisher would like to thank the following for permission to reproduce their material.
Every care has been taken to trace copyright holders. However, if there have been unintentional
omissions or failure to trace copyright holders, we apologize and will, if informed, endeavour
to make corrections in any future edition.

Key: *b* = bottom, *c* = centre, *l* = left, *r* = right, *t* = top

Cover *front cover* Science Photo Library (SPL)/Roger Harris; pages 1 SPL/Sandia National Laboratories; 2–3 National Geographic Society (NGS)/David Lawrence/Panoramic Images; 4–5 NGS/H Takeuchi/Panoramic Images; 7 SPL/Gusto; 8–9 Photolibrary.com; 8*cl* Getty/Photographer's Choice; 9*tr* Corbis/George Shelley; 10–11 SPL/Gusto; 10*tr* SPL/Martin Dohrin; 11*br* SPL/Philippe Psaila; 12–13 Getty/Taxi; 12*tr* SPL; 12*b* Corbis/Bettmann; 13*br* Empics/AP; 14*l* Rex Features; 14*br* The Art Archive; 15*tl* Empics/AP; 15*b* SPL/Publiphoto; 16*tl* Empics/AP; 16*b* Corbis/zefa; 17*b* Alamy; 18*tr* Getty/Digital Vision; 18*bl* Photolibrary.com; 18–19 Alamy/Hugh Threlfall; 19*tr* Rex Features; 19*c* SPL/Leonard Lessin; 19*br* Getty/ AFP; 20–21 Getty/Iconica; 20*tl* Corbis/Bettmann; 20*bl* Getty/Hulton; 20*cr* SPL/Alexander Tsiaras; 21*tl* SPL/Mike Miller; 21*br* SPL/David Parker; 22–23 Kobal; 22*tl* SPL/Adam Hart-Davis; 23*tr* Rex Features; 23*c* Ronald Grant Archive; 23*b* Kobal; 24 SPL; 25 SPL/Hugh Turvey; 26*tl* SPL/Sheila Terry; 26–27 Getty/NGS; 27*t* Getty/Imagebank; 27*br* Getty/Taxi; 28*tl* Topfoto; 28*tr* DK Images; 28–29 Corbis/Schlegelmilch; 28*tl* Getty/Iconica; 29*tr* Corbis/Maxine Hall; 30*bl* Topfoto; 30–31*t* SPL/Christian Darkin; 31*tr* Getty/Imagebank; 31*bl* Alamy/Paul Rapson; 32–33*t* Alamy/Lisa Ryder; 32*bl* Getty/Hulton; 33*tl* Empics/AP; 33*tr* Topfoto; 33*b* Getty News/Andreas Rentz; 34*cr* Getty/Hulton; 34*bl* Rex Features; 34–35 Rex Features; 35*tr* SPL/Andrew Syred; 35*br* Corbis/Reuters; 36 Getty News/Andreas Rentz; 37 SPL/Gusto; 38–39 Corbis/ZUMA; 38*tl* Mary Evans Picture Library; 39*tl* Photolibrary.com; 39*br* Topfoto; 40–41 China Photos; 40*tl* Getty/Hulton; 40*c* Corbis/Sygma; 41*tl* Corbis/zefa; 42–43 Getty/NGS; 42*cl* Ullstein Bild; 42–43*b* Getty/NGS; 43*cr* Topfoto; 43*br* Alamy/Alan Spencer; 44–45 SPL/Victor Habbick Visions; 44*cl* SPL/US Air Force; 44*br* Topfoto; 45*tr* Topfoto; 45*br* Topfoto; 46*tl* SPL/Novosti; 46*b* SPL/NASA; 47*t* Rex Features; 47*b* NASA; 48 Photolibrary.com; 49 SPL/Gusto; 50–51 Getty/Imagebank; 50*tl* Mary Evans Picture Library; 51*tl* SPL/Pascal Goetgheluck; 51*br* Rex Features; 52*tl* Getty News/Joe Raedle; 52*tr* SPL/David Parker; 52*bl* SPL/Eye of Science; 53 SPL/Christian Darkin; 54–55*c* SPL/Eurelios; 54*bl* SPL/Russell Kightley; 55*tr* SPL/Roslin Institute/Eurelios; 55*c* Corbis/Karen Kasmauski; 55*cb* Alamy/Photofusion; 56*c* Photolibrary.com; 56*bl* Rex Features; 56–57*t* Rex Features; 57*cr* Still Pictures; 57*b* Photolibrary.com; 58 Rex Features; 59 Corbis/David Kadlubowski; 60 Corbis/Robert Harding; 61 SPL/Tek Image; 64 Getty/Hulton.